Unbornness

Eine Brücke ist der Mensch
Zwischen dem Vergangnen
Und dem Sein der Zukunft;
Gegenwart ist Augenblick;
Augenblick als Brücke.
Seele gewordner Geist
In der Stoffeshülle
Das ist aus der Vergangenheit;
Geist werdende Seele
In Keimesschalen
Das ist auf dem Zukunftwege.
Fasse Künftiges
Durch Vergangnes

Hoff' auf Werdendes
Durch Gewordenes.
So ergreif das Sein
Im Werden;
So ergreif, was wird
Im Seienden.

Weihnacht, 24. December 1920

Rudolf Steiner

UNBORNNESS

Human Pre-existence
and the Journey toward Birth

PETER SELG

2010
STEINERBOOKS

SteinerBooks
610 Main Street, Great Barrington, MA 01230
www.steinerbooks.org

Translated by Margot M. Saar. Originally published in German by Verlag des Ita Wegman Instituts 2009 as *Ungeborenheit. Die Präexistenz des Menschen und der Weg zur Geburt.*

Library of Congress Cataloging-in-Publication Data

Selg, Peter, 1963-
 [Ungeborenheit. English]
 Unbornness : human pre-existence and the journey toward birth / Peter Selg ; [translated by Margot M. Saar].
     p. cm.
 "Originally published in German by Verlag des Ita Wegman Instituts 2009 as Ungeborenheit. Die Prexistenz des Menschen und der Weg zur Geburt"—T.p. verso.
 Includes bibliographical references and index.
 ISBN 978-0-88010-718-1 (alk. paper)
 1. Pre-existence. 2. Steiner, Rudolf, 1861-1925. 3. Anthroposophy. I. Saar, Margot M. II. Title.
 BD426.S4513 2010
 299'.935—dc22

                                    2010019798

[. . .] We need another word—besides the word "immortality," which denotes the end of physical life—to speak of the eternal, imperishable aspect of the human essence, as opposed to the perishable, transient human body: we need the word "unbornness." For, just as we pass through the gate of death with our eternal, spiritual essence and continue on to another life in the spiritual world—one visible to spiritual investigation—so too, we descend before birth or conception from the spiritual world into physical, earthly incarnation. Not only do we pass through the gate of death as immortal beings, we enter through the gate of birth as unborn beings. We need the term "unbornness," as well as the term "immortality," to encompass the whole human being.

— RUDOLF STEINER[1]

Contents

Preface

Life after death —
Life before birth;
Only by knowing both
Do we know eternity.

— *Rudolf Steiner, dedication, (1914)*[2]

CHILDREN ARE BORN EVERY DAY on every continent and country on earth. They come into the world and begin to breathe on their own. And their arrival, after months of waiting, is sudden and "new." They are newly born, vulnerable, yet enchanting; and truly individual beings. In fact, the "newborn" meet the earthly world with an essential personal dignity, a distinctive I-dimension to their being. Faced with this undeniable truth, we must ask where children or their souls come from, a question that no amount of scientific reductionism and no powerful genetic paradigm has ever managed to silence. From their very first day, children are clearly different from their parents, whom they now meet. They arrive with their own laws of individuality, their own being, and their own history, which reaches far into the past—much farther than the day of their birth and the nine months of pregnancy.

In contrast to the multitude of discussions in medical ethics and the many attempts to establish the exact moment when the embryo must be assigned human dignity, Rudolf Steiner declared categorically that the child's higher individuality steers and determines the entire pregnancy right from the beginning. From the perspective of anthroposophy, the human soul's will to incarnate exists *before* conception takes place and must be taken into consideration if one wants to gain a deeper understanding of the process in its entirety. The question of life before birth, or "unbornness," therefore refers not only to the embryonic-fetal development that takes place before birth, but to the entire existence and history of the human individuality, in its journey from the spiritual world to earth. During the first two decades of the twentieth century, Rudolf Steiner repeatedly explained that a one-sided religious preoccupation with the question of immortality or continued spiritual existence after earthly death meant that the opposite and complementary pole—the question of an individual's existence before birth and, particularly, before conception—was disregarded. Speaking about the history of consciousness and culture, Steiner said in 1920:

> [...] In the period when human beings were able to look toward the divine spiritual world cognitively with moral, religious insight—when they were still able to relate the supersensible in the human being to the supersensible in the world—people asked: How did human beings come down from the spiritual worlds, where they lived before, onto this earth? The natural germinal development before birth was seen as the mere outer expression of this descent from divine spiritual worlds onto the physical plane. Birth was the great mystery. "What is our task here on earth?" Human beings asked themselves. Today when people try to come closer to the great mystery of the true human essence, they focus on the opposite, on death.[3]

"Unbornness," Rudolf Steiner says, is "the other side of eternity." But in today's human consciousness, "unbornness" plays only a marginal part. *We have no idea what we are lacking in this regard.*[4] What is obvious is that this "lack" of insight (or even the lack of questions in this area) seriously affects not only our self-knowledge, but also what we do and refrain from doing in our handling of different situations in life. The field of prenatal diagnostics and intervention appears in a wholly different light when we understand that in the development of each child (including the embryonic-fetal phase) a human individuality is working to enter into and shape a meaningful earthly existence. Throughout the world, innumerable abortions of these journeys take place, carried out because of imagined or actual physical circumstances, initiated by physicians or parents without consideration or respect for the will to incarnate of this individuality, who embarked on its journey in spite of the prevailing obstacles, and maybe even in full knowledge of them. Scientific medicine claims to be free from any particular ideology. Yet, its diagnostic and therapeutic methods obviously rest on premises that are rarely called into question. These premises have to do with the image and essence of the human being, as well as the whole concept of the human body and biography, and therefore also with the origin of the human being.

For Rudolf Steiner, human pre-existence or "unbornness," the knowledge of a life before birth, was not a postulate or a question of belief. It was the result of inner experience—evidence gained by thorough spiritual-scientific research.[5] Rudolf Steiner hoped and expected that a fundamental transformation of thinking would take place in the further evolution of human consciousness—a transformation and extension of thinking that again (and anew) could perceive human life between death and birth as part of a wider biography, including the existence of the human individuality before conception and beyond death. ("Life will only be understood if we see it in its entirety, not if we consider only the short segment of time between birth and death, for that particular segment depends intrinsically on spiritual occurrences before birth. In our entire essence we depend on what happened in the spiritual world before we were born."[6]) According to Rudolf Steiner, ancient human proto-languages still had words that denoted the concept of "unbornness," but these words and concepts later disappeared from human consciousness and from terminology. The following verse of ancient Indian wisdom was translated into German by Rudolf Steiner:

Urselbst,	Primeval self
Von dem alles ausgegangen,	From whom all things derive,
Urselbst,	Primeval self
Zu dem alles zurückkehrt,	To whom all things return,
Urselbst,	Primeval self
Das in mir lebt —	That in me lives —
Zu dir strebe ich hin.[7]	To thee will I aspire.

From the spiritual-scientific perspective, the events or, rather, processes that surround birth (or conception) and death are merely "transformations," shaped and passed through by a human being on his individual journey.[8]

*

Rudolf Steiner wanted the term *Ungeborenheit* ("unbornness") to become accepted; he often said that the concept or word had to be "conquered"[9] by the German language, that it had to be "wrenched" from "temporal and scientific evolution."[10]

> We need the word "unborn." It must become as established a concept in cultural languages as the word "immortal," which already exists in the languages.[11]

We can understand what Rudolf Steiner implied by this and why the development of the word and concept of "unbornness" was so all-important to him: it meant the recognition of the human individuality and of its meaningful, always particular, journey to earth. The objection that a newly introduced word or concept cannot stop difficult, if not destructive tendencies in certain areas of life—tendencies that aim at the veritable elimination of the human individuality, that deny it and obstruct its development—is justified. But it is not helpful. Rudolf Steiner was well aware of this ubiquitous danger and pointed out how important the spirit and content of our language are; and how important what we think and express in language is to counteract other forces and powers.[12] He hoped that the word and concept of "unbornness," would become part of twentieth century culture and civilization—an essential aspect of a new way of thinking about the human being. If such thinking became reality and managed to take hold again of anthropology, of the wider, real life-story of the human being, it would become true knowledge, wisdom of humanity (*anthropo-sophia*), because then the world—how we think about the world and the actions that arise out of this thinking—would be transformed.

If we see children, including newborn children, as individualities who come from a spiritual background and bring with them their specific pre-experiences and missions—who stand at the beginning of an earthly biography chosen by themselves and consciously (or rather, super-consciously) embarked on—this will affect our attitude toward them and also our attitude toward our own selves, which have come to earth under the same circumstances. The question of human immortality and life-after-death often has an egocentric quality. Members of religious denominations tend to rely on it to fill their churches, a fact frequently referred to by Rudolf Steiner. The concept of "unbornness" can overcome this one-sidedness; it focuses on where children come from and tries to do justice to, and understand and share, their individual essence. If selflessly approached and perceived, *both* of these themes or boundary experiences are existential and essential. From this perspective, they no longer ask only about our own essence, but also—and perhaps primarily—about the essence of the other, about the other's own particular path, which we need to understand as a basis for any future community with him or her. To reflect on "unbornness" can be the beginning of this new orientation.

*

The following essay is the slightly extended transcript of a lecture I was invited to give by the association *Geburtshaus an der Ita Wegman Klinik** on May 5, 2009, to support the midwives who, under difficult financial conditions, try their best to maintain the maternity clinic that had been inspired by Ita Wegman herself three years before her death: "This is really something that Dr. Steiner had as an ideal: to receive in the right way the children who are coming into the world; doing so, will at the same time contribute to the improvement of humankind." (June 26, 1940[13]). The lecture was an introduction to the detailed descriptions of human life before birth, or rather before conception, given by Rudolf Steiner, which will form the subject of a comprehensive monograph to be published at a later time.[14] Living with and deeply reflecting on some of the contents and motifs presented by Rudolf Steiner through spiritual science can be an important contribution to the attempt to give new weight and substance to the forgotten concept of "unbornness." This kind of initiative does not, in my opinion, fall so much within the purview of theologians, philosophers, psychologists or ethical committees, but falls primarily within the fields of those who are more intimately involved with the mystery of birth: physicians, midwives and parents, who have their own intuitive insights and are bearers of another, often much more specific, knowledge, including that of the child's real "name." To them, these thoughts are dedicated. *"We must seek the things that are subtle and quiet / and venture forth to gain the light"* (Christian Morgenstern).[15]

I would like to thank Elisabeth Lindenmaier and the midwives of the Arlesheim maternity clinic for inviting me to give this talk, and Walter Schneider who provided a reproduction of the

---

*Maternity clinic at the Ita Wegman Clinic in Arlesheim, Switzerland.

Sistine Madonna for the evening, the image that lends a special mood and spirit to the lecture. In 1943, in the midst of World War II and the year of Ita Wegman's death, Theodor Hetzer, a noted art historian in Germany, wrote that with regard to the *Sistine Madonna* it was important "whether we are able, through observation and understanding, to imbue ourselves with its existence, with its sensory-spiritual essence."[16] Astonished, we discover how much Rudolf Steiner's spiritual-scientific presentations can contribute to this process.

PETER SELG

Director of the Ita Wegman Institute
for Basic Research into Anthroposophy

1.

The *Sistine Madonna* and the *Chorus of the Unborn*

Raffaello Santi and Nelly Sachs

Love most sublime
Like art most sublime
Is devotion.

— JOHANN GOTTFRIED HERDER[17]

Raphael: THE SISTINE MADONNA, 1512-13

At THE AGE OF THIRTY, in the winter of 1512/13, Raffaello Santi painted the *Sistine Madonna* "for the black monks in Piacenza"[18]—that is, for the newly built church of the Benedictine monastery of San Sisto in Rome, which had been consecrated the year before. Thus the *Sistine Madonna* was painted as a high altar picture, a "cultic image" (Hetzer[19]) and was hung behind the altar, the place of the sacrament of Christ. The curtains on the painting are pulled back to reveal an epiphany or vision that "arose from Raphael's entelechy"[20] as an image of devotion. In the words of the poet Herder in his poem on the *Sistine Madonna*: "Love most sublime, like art most sublime/ is devotion."[21] The two figures, to the left and right, the saints Sixtus II and Saint Barbara (to whom the high altar was dedicated) kneel in reverent devotion to the Madonna and child in "exoteric duality"[22]: one gazing upward and the other with her gaze lowered.

Carl Gustav Carus, an enthusiastic observer of the *Sistine Madonna* in Dresden, spoke of the figures' *omnipresence* ("wherever we turn our gaze, the figures stand pure, eye to eye with us").[23] Like many others before and after him, Carus focused in his studies on the mysticism and visionary power of Raphael's creation, its "revelatory," or "appearing," quality (Hetzer[24]). He spoke of its singular genesis: "Through and through, the picture has the character of a work swiftly sketched out of an inner spiritual urgency and quickly executed in the fire of enthusiasm. Pure and large, the figures rose before Raphael's inner eye and were transferred onto the canvas just as they were seen, seemingly without effort, but with great purpose."[25] The overall composition was "of the highest eurythmy," the German writer Alfred von Wolzogen declared in 1865[26] and, in 1955, the art historian Marielene Putscher still wrote about the painting's extraordinary effect:

The picture possesses an immediacy that hardly any other
of Raphael's works has, one that hardly any other painting
achieves: *the immediacy of a sketch*; and yet, in the next
moment, it can appear infinitely removed to a realm of
perfection that is simply out of human reach: *as perfect as
if it were not created by the human hand.*[27]

Twelve years before, in 1943, Theodor Hetzer wrote about
the painting:

We do not ask how Raphael painted it—there are no
known drawings or sketches for it—it stands before us in
perfection, a vision that has become form, spirit that has
become form, and hence *more real* than what is usually
given shape to on canvas through color.[28]

The Madonna, carrying the child, is in the center of the Sistine
painting. In a pronounced manner, she steps forth from the heavenly realm. Hermann Grimm described the Madonna's weight-
less gait as hovering and walking in one, her bare feet touching
the clouds on a path "that is not solid, but still a road."[29] It has
been pointed out repeatedly—by Karl Morgenstern, Hermann
Grimm and Theodor Hetzer among others—that the fold of
Sixtus' cloak and the shadows of the clouds describe a curve
that evokes the image of the globe. "One has a mental image
of the earthly sphere touched by Mary's feet" (Hetzer[30]). With
deep sincerity and love, Mary, surrounded by a bright, radiant
light, carries the Christ child out of the spiritual heavenly realm
toward the earth—down to an abysmal world that awaits him.
As Arthur Schopenhauer wrote at the beginning of his poem *To
the Sistine Madonna*:

She bears him to the world, and startled
He beholds the chaos of its abominations,
The frenzy and fury of its turmoil,

The never-cured folly of its striving,
The never-stilled pain of its distress.[31]

According to Hermann Grimm, Sixtus II and Saint Barbara (both of whom died as martyrs in the third century and whose relics were taken to the monastery of Piacenza in the ninth century) are the advance guard of an expectant humanity. They have ascended "several steps" to the heavenly spheres to receive the Madonna and her child.[32]

The gaze of both Mary and the child is portrayed as deeply serious, but also as loving. Filled with a devotion to the world that rests in the self and returns to the self, they are shown in the gesture and attitude of contemplation and profound knowledge—of past, present, and future. Wilhelm Kelber spoke of the "cosmic earnestness" that lay in the Christ child's eyes and countenance. According to Carus "the most sublime spiritual power of the picture lies in the gaze of these wonderful eyes that is beyond words."[33] Theodor Hetzer likewise remarked a "supernatural power" speaks out of the child's eyes.[34] Regarding the child's posture, Hermann Grimm wrote in a meditation on the *Sistine Madonna*:

> It seems to us as if he were reading his fate out of the air, considering it as if he had already suffered and overcome what still lay far ahead. Unlike the Christ child in the *Madonna della Sedia*, he is not surrounded by dreams, but filled with premonitions of an inevitable, terrible future and determined to face what this future will bring. How the child sits there as if he had no weight for his mother, although he no longer has the body of a newborn baby; how he rests his hand on his comfortably crossed leg; in both these, his posture is that of a person in thought. Here, too, Raphael uses contrast to enhance this impression with the two cherubs at the bottom, representing the thoughtless contentment of infancy. They are not doing anything,

not expecting anything; they know nothing of the past and future. They flutter about in the sunlight, their smiles suggesting future happiness, while their tears suggest the opposite, all for the duration of only a moment—while, in the brow of the Christ child, the contemplation of millennia seems to dwell.[35]

Theodor Hetzer thinks that the faces of Christ child and the Madonna relate to each other like "sun and moon"[36]: that is, they are intimately and essentially related, despite the difference between them. In his 1865 book on Raphael, Alfred von Wolzogen wrote: "If I had to think of another trait that always struck me particularly in this painting, it is the genuinely moving family likeness in the faces of Mary and the child, a likeness that does not in the least compromise the definite difference in the spiritual expression of either [...]."[37] Despite their intimacy and despite Mary's central position, however, the spiritual center of the painting is the child. Embraced and carried by the mother, the Christ approaches the earth. "Despite his childlike appearance the Christ is dominant, while the Madonna does not seem to foster any feelings of her own, but lives in selfless devotion to the 'divine germ' that she envelops and protects" (Wilhelm Kelber[38]). Mary's upper body with the veil and the child describe the perfect shape of a heart.

*

The image of the *Sistine Madonna* is Christological or Christocentric. It depicts Christ's arrival on earth as the son of Mary. Thus, in an archetypal way, it also depicts the secret of every human incarnation. Herder wrote in more general terms: "Each of the madonnas, almost each one of Raphael's figures, is imbued with a spirit that everywhere reveals, even to those most resistant to it, the disposition in human nature that has been described as the angel in humanity."[39] Herder referred to Raphael's figures as "meditative images of pure forms of humanity," and many observers of the *Sistine Madonna* have written about the "wonderful mystery of childhood" (Schlegel) that is revealed in the "divine child" (Carus) by the divine presence "in childlike form": "The mystery of the combination of both natures seems to me best solved in the wonderful mystery of childhood, as such that is as boundless in its essence as it is bounded" (Schlegel).[40] Hegel pointed out:

> Thus Raphael's Christ children, especially the one of the *Sistine Madonna* in Dresden, are of the most beautiful childlike expression, and yet there is in them a transcendence beyond mere childlike innocence that allows us to behold the divine presence in the young shape and to sense the extension of this divinity toward infinite revelation, while the childlike quality, at the same time, provides the justification that such revelation is not yet complete.[41]

In this sense, the Christ child in the *Sistine Madonna* is the representative of childhood and of humankind. The painting shows the mystery of human incarnation—of the guided entrance of divine-spiritual powers into the realm of earthly powers.[42] *"As if gathered from the clouds and embraced, this child appears to us, not as if born of a woman"* (Rudolf Steiner).[43] According to Rudolf Steiner, the clouds in this painting *"really all represent children"*—"so we have the impression that it was through the condensation of a thinner substance that the Madonna received the Jesus child out of the clouds."[44] "It is as if out of the cloud formations one of the angels had solidified and descended down to earth, but all wonderfully raised to a spiritual level."[45] On January 30, 1913, Rudolf Steiner said in Berlin:

> The way the mother walks toward us as one of the most magnificent, most noble pieces of art in the history of humanity; the way she appears to us with the child,

floating toward us on cloudy heights that cover the earthly globe, floating out of the vagueness, one might say, of the spiritual-supersensible world, enveloped and surrounded by clouds that seem to shape themselves into human figures one of whom resembles—as if condensed—the child of the Madonna....[46]

According to Rudolf Steiner, the painting of the *Sistine Madonna* depicts a super-physical birth: the "birth of the soul out of the cloud ether"[47] and not an actual incarnation. Wilhelm Kelber also wrote:

This child is not born. Or rather, it is not the aspect of his birth that is alluded to or portrayed here. He has come out of the ensouled world, which visibly surrounds him in this picture, into Mary's arms.[48]

Understood in this way, the *Sistine Madonna* reveals through the archetypal Christ image an essential mystery of human existence: the journey to the earth of the human soul-spirit, under the protection and guidance of maternal powers, and within the dynamics of a knowing arrival that begins in other spheres. Raphael's *Sistine Madonna* brings to light the special journey of Christ and is determined and shaped by him (as humanity's "higher" or "divine self"[49]). She is therefore at the same time "*a symbol of what is eternally supernatural in the human being and approaches the earth out of the spiritual world, and has beneath it, separated by clouds, all that can emerge only from the earthly realm*" (Rudolf Steiner).[50] Carl Gustav Carus referred to the *Sistine Madonna* as "the first picture in the world."[51]

On April 18, 1926, the young Christian Community priest Eduard Lenz wrote to his wife Friedel Lenz from Dresden:

You see, in truth, the *Sistine Madonna* is entirely different from what one often imagines. What I have experienced is that through the open curtain one beholds, in the imagination, the world of unborn souls. The beings gaze at you out of the azure itself. They flow together into the wonderfully gentle, earthly-ethereal, beautiful figure of the Virgin, who is carrying the child. He is a true Sun child. The gaze of the child is not of this world. There is something about the Virgin carrying the Sun child in her arms that is unsettling. Her step shows a wonderful balance between virginal distance from the earth and maternal-tender closeness to the earth. Her countenance not only has a chaste, ethereal aspect, but at the same time a remarkable experience speaks out of it. The eyes shine with radiant serenity and love—they also gaze as if out of worlds of pain. The eyes of the Madonna are like the eyes of Rudolf Steiner. Remember how he sometimes lifted his gaze in such a heavy way and how a look of infinite goodness met you out of his warm, dark brown eyes, out of a sacrificed life. Then you will know what the gaze of Raphael's Madonna is like. They are really the eyes of Sophia, cosmic Wisdom, consolidated from the worlds of maternal etheric forces. The brown-grey veil, which is wrapped around the Madonna's head, also makes us think of this pain, of the suffering that has been endured. This brown-grey color stands out oddly in the painting. The curse of suffering and darkness is also present in this painting that nevertheless is all radiant luminosity. I want to return often to this picture. The mysteries of the world gaze down on you.[52]

*

During the war, the *Sistine Madonna*, together with many other art treasures, was removed from the Dresden Art Gallery and stored for years in the *Albrechtsburg* in Meissen. On December 15, 1943, it was taken to the Gross-Cotta railway tunnel in the Saxon mountains, code-named "Rescue Site T."[53] Thus, the

Madonna survived the bombing of Dresden on February 13, 1945. The two daughters of Eduard Lenz, Sophie and Ruth, however, perished in the attack. Eduard Lenz himself lost his life in November 1945, as a Soviet prisoner-of-war on a cattle truck, on the way home from the coal mines of Lake Baikal.

Nine months later, in the summer of 1946, in Stockholm, in the Jewish Community House—the shelter for refugees and survivors—Nelly Sachs wrote a cycle of thirteen poems, which she called "Choruses after Midnight" (Chöre nach der Mitternacht). It was published in East Berlin, in 1947, in her first post-war volume of poetry *In the Dwellings of Death (In den Wohnungen des Todes)*, which she dedicated to "my dead brothers and sisters." Leading up to the cycle's final poem "Voice of the Holy Land" Nelly Sachs let thirteen choruses, witnesses of what happened, resound: "In the choruses, what remained after the Shoah—namely, wounded, shattered, and orphaned things and people—finds words to speak." The choruses were the "Chorus of Things Left Behind," "Chorus of the Rescued," "Chorus of Wanderers," "Chorus of Orphans," "Chorus of the Dead," "Chorus of the Shadows," "Chorus of the Stones," "Chorus of the Stars," "Chorus of Things Invisible," "Chorus of the Clouds," "Chorus of the Trees," "Chorus of the Comforters," and finally, in thirteenth place, "Chorus of the Unborn":

Chorus of the Unborn

We the unborn:
Already longing starts to work on us,
The shores of blood widen in welcome,
And we sink into love like dew.
Yet time's shadows still lie like questions
Over our secret.

You lovers
Full of yearning,

And sick with farewell, listen:
It is we who begin to live in your glances,
In your hands that seek in the azure blue;
It is we who bear the fragrance of morning.
Already your breath is drawing us in,
Admitting us into the depths of your slumber,
Into your dreams, our kingdom on earth,
Where our black wet-nurse, the night,
Will let us grow
Until your eyes mirror us,
Until our voices speak in your ears.

Butterfly-like,
We are caught by the clasps of your longing—
And sold to the earth like the singing of birds—
Fragrant with morning,
We are lights that approach to illumine your sadness.[55]

Many observers of the Sistine Madonna have felt, like Eduard Lenz, that the children's faces in the painting's spiritual background and periphery were not angels but human souls waiting to enter earthly existence in order to embark on their life journey: the clouds in the painting are *"really all children,"* Rudolf Steiner said. *"They are the hosts of the unborn drawn towards life by the Madonna,"* wrote Oswald Spengler.[56] In the middle of the 20th century, having witnessed the most horrendous destruction, a Jewish survivor wrote about these "unborn" beings and their journey toward birth. Unlike Raphael, Nelly Sachs followed them right into the sphere of the body, the physiological sphere. She spoke of the widening "shores of blood" and of growth in the night of the maternal body, in concealment. The souls of the unborn are drawn toward the earth by the powerful longing of lovers, by their inspiration ("already your breath is drawing us in"). The parents' longing is creative, active ("already longing starts to work on us"). Thus, creatively, something new begins in the human sphere. Despite the gravity of history, the burden of time, a "light approaches." The unborn who "bear the fragrance of morning" come down to the earth, to the realm of the visible and audible, the sphere of earthly life and human encounter, between I and you ("until your eyes mirror us, until our voices speak in your ears").

Just after World War II, children were being born into ruined cities and traumatized families, into "time's shadows" and their "sadness." Nelly Sachs knew the situation of many newborn children, whose fathers had fallen in the war, yet who still came to the earth. She knew of many children who had found their way to earth in the middle of the war, under the most adverse circumstances: in the concentration camp of Auschwitz and in the shacks of Birkenau, three thousand children were born, and only few of them survived their first few days. In 1946, Nelly Sachs let speak the "Chorus of the Unborn," the chorus of those who "bear the fragrance of morning," as they face the past and the coming, already dawning future.

The *Sistine Madonna* and the *Chorus of the Unborn* speak in color and word, in form and sound, of the human soul's journey to the earth: of the mystery of the process of human incarnation. Raphael's painting is about the journey of Christ as the representative of humankind. It is about a journey to the earth and into the sphere of death—a journey undertaken in full awareness, in full knowledge of future suffering and of its deeper meaning— a journey whose acceptance and overcoming characterize the Mystery of Golgotha. Nelly Sachs in her way also wrote about, and out of, the sphere of unbornness. She wrote of the sinking "dew" for which the earth longs and of the approaching light, which human beings attract with their love. Although she had a strongly developed sense of self and of individuality,[57] this did not enter into her poem.

Through her friend Gudrun Dähnert, who saved her life, Nelly Sachs knew of Rudolf Steiner's anthroposophical work, including his teachings on incarnation and reincarnation. In contrast to her poem's focus on conception as the response to the longing to which the unborn surrender ("Butterfly-like / We are caught in the clasp of your longing"), Rudolf Steiner spoke of the voluntary journey of the unborn to the earth, of the individual dimension of destiny of human souls, each of which arrives on earth and is born into a meaningful life.

2.

The Human Soul and the Cosmos

Life before Conception

Considering in this way what human beings experience between death and a new birth, a feeling of human responsibility can develop that tells us: If you assess the whole meaning of what it is to be a human being on the basis of what the gods achieve in their work on the human being between death and a new birth, then you must also work hard to deserve to be a human being in earthly life.

— RUDOLF STEINER [58]

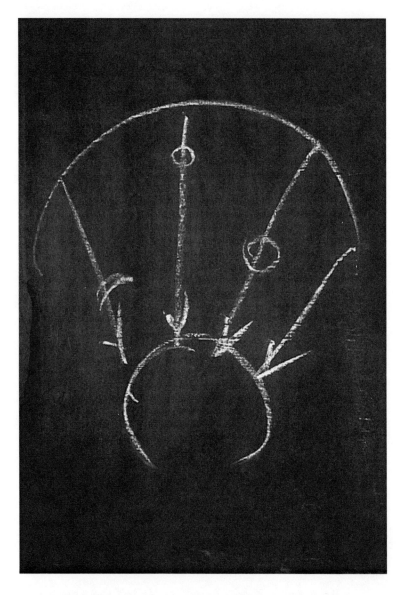

Rudolf Steiner: blackboard drawing, January 4, 1924.
From: Rudolf Steiner, *Wandtafelzeichnungen zum Vortragswerk*,
vol. 23, p. 14, extract. © Rudolf Steiner Archives, Dornach

This is the most radical thought that must arouse humanity today: namely, we must not only see our physical life as a preparation for life after death, but we must also see it as the continuation of a spiritual life before birth. A lazy, idle person will then change and become aware that he or she has a task to fulfil, a mission on earth. Human beings will sink deeply into materialism if they are not entirely penetrated by this thought.[59]

For RUDOLF STEINER, the I, the *eternal foundation* of the human being, is not on earth just once but often—suffering and shaping its destiny as part of its further development, compensating for what was not achieved in the past—in the space between I and You, in the work on earth.

Unlike today in the twenty-first century, the idea of reincarnation was hardly acceptable in society in Rudolf Steiner's times. It was nevertheless one of his innermost life tasks to develop, formulate, and represent a detailed doctrine of incarnation and reincarnation. "Reincarnation and Karma and Their Significance for Present Culture"[60] was the title he chose for a series of lectures on the theme and, as early as 1904, he published a remarkable chapter in his fundamental work *Theosophy*, entitled: "Destiny and the Reincarnation of the Spirit" in which he concluded, after a description that is as subtle as it is comprehensive:

The course of a human life within the framework of life and death is determined in three different ways, and we are also therefore dependent on three factors that go beyond birth and death. The body is subject to the law of *heredity*; the soul is subject to self-created destiny or, to use an ancient term, to its *karma*; and spirit is subject to the laws of *reincarnation* or repeated earthly lives.[61]

The human individuality, the individual spirit, turns repeatedly to the earth to incarnate in a body, in a family, a country, and a time. Incarnated, the I realizes its earthly biography in experiences and events that are part of its destiny. At the same time, it creates this destiny anew in its soul-spirit existence. In returning to the earth, the soul seeks out compensatory and corrective experiences that are the consequences and results of its former earthly life. Therefore, it also seeks out the human beings with whom it was once associated, so as to become actively involved with them and on them in the form of their relationship and their working together. "Human beings with whom the soul was connected in one life must be found again in a following life, because what has happened between them must have consequences. Just like this one soul, all the souls that have a connection with it will seek to reincarnate at a particular time. The soul's life is thus a result of the destiny created by the human spirit" (Rudolf Steiner).[62]

> Present longing shall grow to will,
> And present will to strength will turn
> After the quiet so rich and still.
> Strength creating what is willed,
> Will that out of this creating
> Gives new momentum, bears us on.
> Christian Morgenstern[63]

The human spirit, according to Rudolf Steiner, comes to earth to actively gain experiences and undergo transformations that can be achieved only on earth. This process of inner growth and maturation is the purpose of our earthly existence. It is the mission and meaning of incarnation—a development that proceeds through joy and sorrow, work and meaningful activity, and through human encounters. Rudolf Steiner once said to the teachers of the Stuttgart Waldorf School:

> *We want to work by letting flow into our work what, out of the spiritual world, through soul, body, and spirit, strives to become human in us.*[64]

*

Rudolf Steiner described how long periods of time—many centuries, often more than a millennium—lie between two incarnations. The individual spirit-soul returns only when conditions, culture, and life on earth have fundamentally changed so as to provide a context in which a particular biography can and must unfold in a new way. Between incarnations, the human individuality lives in the cosmos—not physically speaking in empty space, but in pure time, in different spheres of energy and encounter, which are determined and permeated by a high spirituality.

The detachment from earthly conditions through death at the end of one life is not easy and requires a long process of "dehabituation." At the beginning of 1912 Rainer Maria Rilke wrote at Duino Castle:

> It is truly strange to no longer inhabit the earth,
> to no longer practice customs barely acquired,
> not to give a meaning of human futurity
> to roses, and other expressly promising things:
> no longer to be what one was in endlessly anxious hands,
> and to set aside even one's own
> proper name like a broken plaything.
> Strange: not to go on wishing one's wishes. Strange
> to see all that was once in place, floating
> so loosely in space. And it's hard being dead,
> and full of retrieval, before one gradually feels
> a little eternity....[65]

On the basis of his spiritual-scientific research Rudolf Steiner described this process in great detail.[66] He described the human being "detaching" from the earth,[67] and also the process of "retrieval" (Rilke). During the first phase after death, which often stretches over decades, the human soul actually relives its biography in reverse order from death back to birth, while experiencing it from the point of view of others, the environment, and the people on whose lives it made an impact in a good way or a bad way, causing joy or pain. The inner view of one's own life and the focus on one's own perceptions and perspectives become those of the environment—of the social sphere. The experiences gained here are intense, *"so that this life after death [...] is inwardly experienced by human beings in a more substantial, realistic way than life on earth, which is like a dream."*[68] These events, right at the beginning of the journey away from earthly life, already connect the human spirit-soul to the earth. According to Rudolf Steiner, it is at this time already that the departed soul develops a "powerful desire"[69] to compensate in the future for everything that was not achieved or was left undone, for pain that was inflicted, or for failures that now confront the soul in the souls of the others. This "desire" passes through different stages and changes over the following decades and centuries, although it is already a firm "decision" at the end of the first phase after death.

Rudolf Steiner described that the "retrieval" from the experience of others occurs in the "lunar sphere," i.e., in a world whose powers are associated with the essence of the "cosmic Moon," but are not identical with its spatial extension. The human soul's journey from the earth into the cosmos passes through different "spheres" as part of a gradual and expanding process. This is also an inner experience.

"We gradually expand into the spheres of the world. What we experience as our self becomes greater and greater."[70] In the incarnated state on earth, human consciousness is bound to the body and determined by the body. Consciousness is an "organ consciousness." It largely identifies with the body: "my heart," "my lungs." The soul's journey into the cosmos, conversely, leads to a continuously expanding peripheral consciousness that knows itself to be one with the spheres of power through which the soul passes and in which it lives. At the same time, this journey is also a growing into the dimension of the hierarchies—from the Angeloi to the Seraphim—that is, into the realm of high spiritual beings, which carry and determine the cosmos. These spiritual hierarchies are centrally involved—evaluating, transforming, and creating—in shaping the human soul's "biography" after death. When, in connection with the soul's earlier passage through the lunar sphere, Rudolf Steiner spoke of a "cosmic evaluation" of human deeds, he also pointed out that human beings had to leave their unjust deeds—the results of their weaknesses and errors, and even their "evilness"—behind in that sphere. The process of penetrating into the cosmos and its spirituality is therefore one of purification and of departure and renunciation. What human beings shed in the sphere of the "Moon" and during the subsequent "Mercury" phase are aspects of their own essence, even if these aspects belong to the shadow realm of their own existence. Passing through the "Mercury" region, they shed what illnesses they suffered and endured as part of their last earthly biography, as well as the consequences imprinted into their body and soul. Separated from the "weaknesses of evil" and the "weaknesses of illness," they then reach, as Rudolf Steiner described, the sphere of "Venus," the element of purest love, of which—as truly "mutilated human beings"—they are in dire need in order to be able to continue on their way toward the spiritual Sun, where they will remain active for most of their time after death (and before a new birth).

Not only everything that was and is good in a human being's essence, but also what was rudimentarily good in his or her earthly life—and yet remained only a good intention and was not yet realized—is enhanced in the "Sun" sphere:

In the Sun sphere, everything that the human being carried in the smallest thought as a good intention begins to become reality and is beheld by the Exusiai, Dynamis, and Kyriotetes. The spiritual entities of the Sun region now behold what was good in one's thoughts, feelings, and experiences. [...] Thus goodness becomes reality in the Sun world through our living together with these entities. We do not understand the language of these entities if we have not thought good thoughts. We cannot stand before them if we have not done good deeds. In the region of the Sun our goodness becomes reality.[71]

The Sun is the sphere of the future and freedom. It is the realm of the second hierarchy, which is closely connected with the Christ being. *"The Sun sphere is pure goodness, radiating, shining goodness. Evil has no place here."* [72]

*

Earthly human life is extremely short compared to the long periods of time between death and a new birth. Each life is also unique, and creates the preconditions for the purely spiritual existence that the human soul experiences in the cosmos. Rudolf Steiner pointed out that the soul prepares its future destiny in the realm of the Sun not just with the beings of the second hierarchy—the Kyriotetes (Dominions), Dynamis (Virtues), and Exusiai (Powers) of Christian esoteric terminology—but also with those "dead" human beings with whom it has a connection. In the sphere of the spiritual Sun, a "pattern and archetype" is fashioned of the soul's next earthly existence,[73] that is, of its future physical body and life constellations.

Rudolf Steiner spoke often and emphatically about the spiritual formation of the new physical body—of its archetype and pattern, which will gain earthly substance only many centuries later, following conception. "However strange this might seem to you: this weaving of the physical human body as a spiritual germ out of the cosmos is the greatest and most important task imaginable in the higher spheres [...] For, however little it might be recognized by the ordinary human mind on earth, the human body is indeed the most complicated structure that exists in the cosmos."[74] "[...] There is no process more sublime in the order of worlds than weaving the human being out of all the world's ingredients."[75] "Great and majestic is the work on the mystery of the human being that human beings, in association with the higher spiritual beings, carry out there."[76]

The spirit form of the human body (which Rudolf Steiner called the "spirit-germ" as opposed to the physical germ provided by the parents) is an "immense fabric of cosmic grandeur and magnificence," which has to be created. (*"We weave humanity out of the cosmos."*[77]) Human beings cannot achieve it by themselves, but the soul of the individuality who died on earth is actively involved in the creative process, together with the spirituality of the cosmos, in "blissful work."[78] Rudolf Steiner wrote:

> During pre-earthly existence, we experience the cosmic creation that is the spirit-germ of our future physical organism. And this spiritual creation is experienced as a unity with the entire spiritual cosmos, while at the same time revealing itself as the cosmic body of the human essence. Our entire existence consists in that we experience *ourselves* in this cosmos. But we do not experience *only* ourselves. Unlike our future physical organism, this cosmic existence does not separate us from the rest of cosmic life. We experience this life as intuition. The life of the other spiritual beings is also *our* life.
>
> As human beings, we live our pre-earthly existence in the active experience of the spirit-germ of our future physical organism. We ourselves prepare this organism in that we collaborate on the spirit-germ with other spiritual

beings in the spiritual world. Just as in earthly life we perceive through our senses a physical environment in which we are active, we perceive in our pre-earthly existence how our physical organism is formed out of the spirit. We are actively involved in its formation, just as during our physical existence we participate actively in the formation of physical things in the world around us.[79]

The human form, which is fashioned in this way, centers on the head and carries the qualities of humanity. For Rudolf Steiner, the "spirit-germ"—the "physical organism created out of the spirit"— as a spiritual archetype of the physical body, is universal and supra-individual, although it has to be newly configured or "woven" in the creation of each human existence. The spirit-germ gains individuality only gradually as it passes through further cosmic stages to become the bearer of a specific future earthly existence.

*

It is in the "Sun sphere," as Rudolf Steiner described in lectures given in 1924, that, as human beings, we experience not only the configuration of our own spirit-body, but also aspects of our future lives, actions, and sufferings. We witness how the spirits of the first hierarchy—the Seraphim, Cherubim and Thrones—present our karma and its consequences in archetypal images. We live through our future lives in the form of the archetypes of our moral earthly existence, of our future karma, *in these beings*, in their "divine patterns." "Seraphim, Cherubim, and Thrones live through what will become our destiny when we descend to earth again. They live through what we will realize as our destiny."[80] We see our future in "the deeds of gods," in images that are not coercive and leave us free. At the same time the willingness is born—and develops in us—to accept this destiny as our own:

We take our karma and how it will come to pass upon us because we first behold it in the "divine deeds" of the Seraphim, Cherubim and Thrones.[81]

The destiny-forming powers are then transformed and woven into the emerging spirit-body and its life-constellations as capacities, talents, and the willingness to realize this destiny. This is a long and subtle process in which other planetary spheres and spiritual beings, from "Mars" to "Saturn," are involved.

*

Nelly Sachs wrote "Choruses after Midnight" in 1946. Decades before, Rudolf Steiner had referred to the turning point of our after-death, cosmic "biography" and the beginning of our new journey to the earth as the *cosmic midnight.*" Halfway through the life-after-death, when all experiences and consequences of the last earthly existence have been transformed and become part of the cosmos, the return journey, the re-orientation toward the earth, begins. "And the point in time has come when one must seek the transition from death to a new birth, from *the human being becoming cosmos to the cosmos becoming a human being.*"[82] Up to this point, the human soul has become more and more alienated from the earth, living entirely into the spiritual cosmos—experiencing with bright, intuitive awareness the reality of the hierarchies, their beings and powers from within. Now, a new longing for the earth arises—a "hunger for heaviness"[83]— accompanied by the feeling, "I must become human again."[84]

The experience of the spiritual beings of the cosmos then gradually weakens over long periods of time. What used to be a real, intuitive encounter becomes mere revelation, a faint reflection. At the same time, the human sense of individuality grows stronger: the emerging and increasing sense of self is an essential part of the search for a new earthly existence. ("With this awakening of the sense of self the need for a new earthly life arises."[85]) A new "interest in the earthly world" is awakened in a particular way:

> We begin to develop an interest in particular human beings who are down below on the earth and also in their children and the children of their children. While previously we had only a heavenly interest, now as the spiritual world becomes revelation, we develop a remarkable interest in certain sequences of generations. They are the sequences of generations at the end of which we find the parents who will give birth to us when we descend once more to earth. But we develop an interest in their ancestors long before that. We follow the generations right down to our parents, and not only chronologically. When this revelation first presents itself we see the entire sequence of generations as in a prophecy.[86]

In the cosmos the human soul connects with the intensely observed sequence of generations into which it will incarnate many centuries later: "for a long time the human soul has been entering into a connection with the generations that will bring forth its future parents. Connecting not only with the great-great-grandparents, but even much earlier in the sequence of generations, the human soul looks down to its forefathers and becomes part of their orientation, of the stream that runs through the generations of its ancestors."[87] On March 7, 1916, Rudolf Steiner said in Berlin:

> [...] You can really imagine it in the following way: the individuality that is going to be born has parents; the parents have parents; and these parents also have parents. Imagine the breadth that opens up as you move back through thirty generations. If you followed thirty generations in this way you would find that many people already

carry the tendencies that will eventually result in bringing man A and woman B together who will then give existence to a human being. And if things had not evolved in this way through the thirty generations, if people had not always married so that in the end A and B could come together, then this dyad, which the human being needs in order to descend into physical incarnation, would not have emerged. In this whole collaboration of many human beings that will eventually bring about the relationship of a particular couple, the spiritual world is at work for the sake of this particular individuality. If, then, we recognize traits of the son in his father or mother, and father and mother again have traits that go back to grandfather and grandmother, great-grandfather and great-grandmother, and so forth, this is because the individuality who is born centuries later, looked down to the great-great-great-grandfather and the great-great-great-grandmother and the thirty generations along the line and formed a plan according to which people would find each other through the generations. All that is already at work. And the inherited similarities are due to the spiritual power that worked down through thirty generations and that will ultimately manifest in a particular human being; it works in father, mother, grandfather, grandmother, great-grandfather, great-grandmother, providing the traits that ultimately must come out. It is not the physical stream that is responsible for the inheritance. The inheritance has been implanted into the physical stream as I have described. The truth is the opposite of what is being claimed by natural science with regard to physical inheritance.[88]

The cosmic individuality "directs" the attributes of the human beings who will later become its earthly "ancestors" from the spiritual world. ("Goethe, to use this example, possessed the attributes of his ancestors because he had been constantly active from the spiritual world implanting his attributes into his fore-fathers."[89]) The I not only incorporates karmic elements into its spirit-germ, but also incorporates them into the hereditary stream of which it will one day be a part, or, in other words, which will provide the abilities and talents (or idiosyncrasies and weaknesses) that it needs to realize its destiny. According to Rudolf Steiner, before the individuality, guided by high spiritual beings, found its family and future parents, it had already decided on the time and place (or nationality) of its next incarnation. What is therefore of central importance is the relationship, chosen and predetermined by the individuality, to the future parents: to the couple to whom the human being feels affectionately drawn, who "will be able to give him the physical shell best suited to the archetype of his future earthly life that was created in the spiritual world."[90] According to Rudolf Steiner, the child, or the individuality who will be born as the child, is actively involved in bringing the parents together (*"The individual on the way to incarnation brings the lovers together."*[91]) The child brings about their connection and makes it possible. "We sink into love like dew," Nelly Sachs wrote of the "unborn." The "love" and "longing" of the parents for each other, which is a prerequisite for conception—"Butterfly-like/We are caught in the clasps of your longing"—is co-created and co-shaped by the child's approaching individuality. It is an aspect of *the child's* love for the parents. Rudolf Steiner said that the "future" child loves the parents long before conception:

> *The love of the parents is [...] the response to the love of the child. It is requited love.*[92]

The journey of a human being to the earth is not smooth, but lined with obstacles and difficulties. Before birth, complex and even harsh biographies are arranged, including countless circumstances of illness, which must occur later, so that something essential may be endured and overcome.[93] The "choice of parents" may also result from an inner struggle, and need to be affirmed and accepted through inner struggle as an aspect of the situation and conditions of one's own destiny:

> A soul on its way to incarnation knows, for example, that it will need a certain kind of education for its next earthly life, a certain kind of knowledge, which it must acquire at an early age. Now it realizes: Yes, there and then I will be able to gain such knowledge. Often this is possible only by renouncing those parents who would offer a happy existence in other respects and deciding for those who cannot provide a happy life. If one had chosen another couple, one would have to say to oneself: Now I cannot achieve precisely what is most important. We should not imagine that everything in spiritual life is so different from what it is on earth. One might see souls who are severely struggling before birth; a soul who says to itself: I might suffer abuse as a child from cruel parents. If a soul finds itself in such a situation, then there will be tremendous inner struggles. One sees, in the case of many souls in the spiritual world who are preparing for birth, how they are faced with these horrendous struggles.[94]

The doctrine of incarnation and reincarnation, as taught by anthroposophical spiritual science, does not imply any smooth "harmonizing" or resolution of difficult, hard-to-understand earthly biographies, which can be marked by violence and neglect, abuse and disturbance. And yet, the life circumstances that emerge are anything but "accidental" or arbitrary. For Rudolf Steiner, the willingness of souls to incarnate into difficult situations was achieved before birth only with great difficulty, a fact that needs to be taken into account when we consider an individual biography. ("One sees, in the case of many souls in the spiritual world who are preparing for birth, how they are faced with these horrendous struggles.") Thus the soul approaches the earth, the human world, after a long time in the cosmos and a period of preparation whose dimensions and quality go far beyond the possibilities of earthly experience. Whatever outer appearance might suggest, the "lights that approach" (Nelly Sachs) come deliberately, out of their own free will.

3.

"From Spiritual to Earthly Community"

Entering Earthly Existence

When we look at birth or at the powerful forces at work in embryonic life between conception and actual birth, we see how what was human spirit-soul is now drawn toward matter. Spirit and soul become inherent to matter. This is a truly complicated process whose deeper significance has not yet been studied in the right way by physiology.

— RUDOLF STEINER[95]

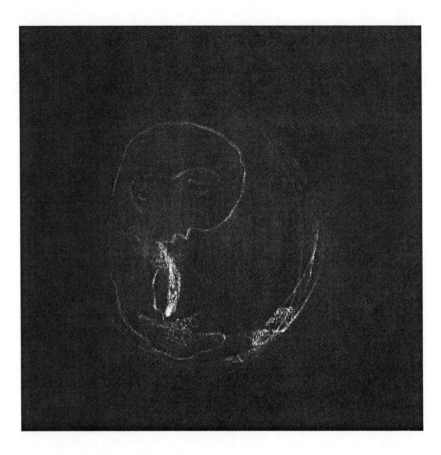

Rudolf Steiner: blackboard drawing. Dornach, January 27, 1923.
From: Rudolf Steiner, *Wandtafelzeichungen zum Vortragswerk*,
volume 25, p. 58. ©Rudolf Steiner Archives, Dornach.

T HE FATHER'S AND MOTHER'S highly polarized gametes or germ cells, which live only for 24 to 36 hours, unite in the process of conception, and thereby initiate the formation of a protective "etheric membrane."[96] Hence the gametes are protected from the material destructiveness of the earth-forces to which they were formerly subject. Through their union—at a state of maximum degeneration, that is, of a highly intensified process of disintegration[97]—they become susceptible to the influence of cosmic powers, of a periph-eral-cosmic impact, [98] namely, the implanting of the "spirit-germ": *"Physical matter is completely destroyed so that the spiritual germ can sink into it and it can become the reflection of the spiritual germ, which was woven out of the cosmos."*[99] *"Fertilization provides only the impulse that causes a certain effect from the cosmos to occur in the human body."*[100] Thus, in the field of tension between the breaking-down processes and the up-building processes, between destruction and life, a tremendous cosmic effect occurs in the smallest physical space. And after centuries of preparation, the physical con-figuration of a macrocosmic form now begins in the earthly realm:

> We might say: the form of the human being is implanted into the womb. In the womb the bed is merely prepared for the human being, and it is a law of the universe that where an opportunity is created for a particular event to take place, this particular event will take place.[101]

The implanting of the spirit-germ into the physical human germ, the fertilized egg, means that a connection is established between the cosmic spirit-form of the physical body and the reproductive stream that the individuality has observed and influenced over a long period of time. Now, from the moment

of conception on, the spirit-germ, which was previously macrocosmic and now infinitely reduced in size and condensed, forms
the element of growth and the "directing power" of the physical
germ, the developing embryo.[102]

*

Although they remain inherently connected, the "spirit-germ"
of the physical body is not identical with the individuality of the
incarnating human being. Together with high spiritual powers,
this individuality worked on the archetype of the physical body
for a new incarnation. But, approaching the earth, at the moment
of conception, the spiritual form of the new physical body "fell
away" from it. "The spirit-germ that we ourselves have woven
is lost to us at the moment when conception takes place on earth
for the physical germ...."[103] In fact, according to Rudolf Steiner,
the progress of the spirit-germ toward the earth accelerates and it
unites with the genetic stream of the physical germ, the fertilized
egg. It lives into the reproductive stream of the parents, while the
human spirit-soul remains in the "lunar sphere," where it pulls
together its etheric body out of the "ingredients of the world
ether." The etheric body is the organism that will later enable
it to enter into a connection with the developing physical germ:
"[...] We are left behind as a spirit-soul being, which feels an
affinity to what has fallen away from it, but is not immediately
able to unite with it. *It can unite with it only if, in this state, it
now contracts into its etheric body the ether forces, which are
in the entire cosmos.*"[104] "The human being clothes itself in its
etheric organism."[105] Rudolf Steiner described how this process
is initiated by the "deprivation," which the individuality experiences because of the departure of the spiritual germ.

Although events occur quickly in the lunar sphere, they are
of immense significance for the new earthly biography. In its
renewed passage through the lunar sphere, the human soul—
the I and the astral body—not only gathers around it its etheric

life-organism, but also undergoes important developments and inner experiences. The brilliance of the cosmic consciousness, which had become progressively weaker during the preceding period, is finally "dimmed down" to the kind of dream consciousness that is both necessary for, and characteristic of, the beginning of the earthly journey. At the same time, the individuality reunites with the burden of "evil" and error that it had left behind in the lunar sphere during the first phase after death, following its separation from its former earthly body. ("[...] Before we unite with our physical germ, we form our ether body [...]. And into this ether body the little package is woven [...] that contains the moral values. This we now weave into our I, into our astral body, and also into our etheric body. We then bring it together with the physical body and in so doing we carry our karma to the earth."[106]) The Moon sphere is, according to Rudolf Steiner, in certain respects the "gateway" of that past,[107] which now must be integrated and transformed.

> I would like to say: the finishing touches come only when we find again our own evilness when we pass through the sphere of the Moon the second time. And then we also add to the intention—to what is to be worked through in the archetypal image—the power to plunge into the karma of a new earthly life.[108]

During this time, in the final weeks before entering the physical world, the individuality has to find the strength that will enable it to truly accept its destiny and "plunge" into its karma. It has to develop the future-oriented longing to realize and advance its karma on earth. Here, in the lunar sphere, the decision is made as to which gender is best suited to the fulfilment of the individual destiny.

United with the etheric body, as its body of time and destiny, the individuality gains a "vision of the future," a preview of its future earthly existence:

When the individuality now connects with the future etheric body, a moment of vision occurs, like the review over the past life after death. But it presents itself in a different way: as a vision of the future, a foresight.[109]

Just as the memories of one's past life rise as a tableau before the soul just after death, a kind of preview of future life precedes the new incarnation. We do not see every detail, but a rough outline of all the circumstances of the life to come. This moment is immensely important. It can even happen that those who endured a great deal in an earlier life, and experienced great hardship, suffer a shock when they perceive their new situation and destiny, and therefore keep their soul from fully incarnating so that only a part of the soul enters into the body.[110]

The *after-death* tableau-like review of earthly life, which extends through the three days of the separation from the etheric body, is characterized by a great, objective supra-personal calmness. As Rudolf Steiner said: "It is characteristic of this tableau that, because of the way it presents itself immediately after death, all subjective experiences of the human being during its time on earth are deleted from the tableau. Our experiences are always accompanied by feelings of pleasure or pain, joy or sadness. But the joys and pains that are attached to the images of life are not part of this review. We stand as objectively before this memory tableau as we stand before a painting. If it presents a person who is sad or full of pain, we look at the person objectively. Although we can sympathize with the sadness, we do not feel the actual pain that this person felt."[111]

In contrast, the preview of the earthly biography, which occurs during the passage through the lunar sphere when the soul is approaching the earth—that is, during the first three weeks after conception—directly affects the soul of the incarnating individuality. The preview does not have the same finality and supra-personal detachment that characterized the after-death etheric review. It can induce a severe sense of shock. Rudolf Steiner spoke of potential constitutional defects and illnesses resulting from this situation, caused by the incomplete penetration of the physical body and manifesting in epileptic fits or impaired mental development.[112]

On the other hand, the soul on its way to incarnation also receives assistance in the earth's etheric membrane. As Rudolf Steiner often described, it is here that the Christ's etheric essence has dwelled since the Mystery of Golgotha. The human soul encounters the Christ immediately after death, when the etheric body is left behind, but also benefits from his help, support and guidance before it embarks on its new earthly journey.

*

The lunar sphere reaches from the earth to the orbit of the physical moon. As Rudolf Steiner pointed out in a presentation on embryology, the higher members of a child's organization are already "close to the mother"[113] when conception takes place. Fallen away from the individuality, the spirit-germ unites with the physical germ at the moment of conception. Nevertheless, the child's spirit-soul, its I and soul-body, which are still part of the "lunar sphere" and "free in the cosmos,[114] are not far removed in terms of spatial distance from the physical human germ. Yet they are not actively and intrinsically involved in the events that take place during the first weeks, the initial germinating process. ("Although from the moment of conception this human being, who consists of I, astral body, and ether body, is close to the mother, who carries the fertilized germ within her, it is active only from the outside."[115] According to Rudolf Steiner, throughout the nine months of pregnancy, the forces continue to work in this way while at the same time a process of modification and differentiation takes place: the higher members of the child's organisation work on the germ "from the outside."

They live and are active in the enveloping organs of the embryo and foetus, in the polarity of inner and outer space—of self-orientation and world-orientation—that has been present from the beginning. Speaking to medical students and physicians in April 1924, Rudolf Steiner emphasized:

> So that, with reference to the physical embryo, we must say: this physical part of the embryo is truly wonderfully formed, but the pre-earthly individuality had little to do with that. The human being—the pre-earthly human being—is involved mostly with what is around the embryo. That is where the pre-earthly human being lives, in what is in fact being broken down in the physical and is discarded as broken down substance, chorion, amnion, and so on.[116]

Rudolf Steiner spoke in a similar way in a presentation on embryology to theologians:

> When we look at birth or at the powerful forces at work in embryonic life between conception and actual birth, we see how what was human spirit-soul is now drawn toward matter. Spirit and soul become inherent in matter. This is a truly complicated process, whose deeper significance physiology has not yet studied in the right way. The development of the germ is, in fact, studied only incompletely. One usually just learns that it starts with the zygote, with the formation of the zygote and its division. In short, one follows the evolution from the first zygote through its different developmental stages until the embryo has reached maturity and is born—but one does not simultaneously follow the development of the chorion, amnion, and the organs that surround the embryo in the womb. They are most perfect at the beginning of embryogenesis, and gain in complexity and are expelled when the embryo is born. The germinal development is in fact an ascending

evolution; while involution occurs as the human spirit-soul gradually moves from the organs of the maternal organism in which it first established itself, from the chorion, from the amnion, into the actual human germ, the embryo itself. This is the involution of spirit-soul into matter. The matter is cast off and what follows it is the evolution of the embryo.[117]

The individuality, the spirit-soul of the child, works from the "outside," as Rudolf Steiner said, through the organs that envelop embryo and fetus. From there, the higher members "gradually" work on the inner germ and transfer, in Steiner's words, into "the actual human germ." In his very early anthroposophical lectures Rudolf Steiner often spoke of the moment, around the end of the third week, when the individuality enters into the physical process of the development of the germ.[118] Around the twenty-first day after conception, the embryo's heart begins to beat and thus the organ of the heart—which relates to the human individuality like no other organ—takes up its activity in the process of incarnation, as it also will do during the process of excarnation when the earthly life comes to an end.[119] The heart is in a very specific way the organ of destiny for human existence—the first functional organ system of the embryonic organism, which Aristotle had already studied in depth and which forms the center of the anthropology of the New Testament.[120]

*

Through the connection of the higher members of the human being, especially the etheric body, with the physical germ, a definite process of individualization takes place in the developing embryonic organization. The etheric time-body carries within it the dimension of destiny: the memory of the last life, its errors and failures, and also the motives and forces of transformation and adjustment. ("How the etheric body with all its vitality is received by the human being depends on how the human being, arriving from pre-earthly existence with its karma, is able to receive it."[121])

All this is now incorporated into the embryonic structure and substance and begins to transform them. ("The physical body only becomes individualized when the ether body penetrates it."[122]) Despite their increasing connection with the physical embryo, the higher members of the human organization continue to prevail in the organs that envelop the embryo after the third week. Here, in the space surrounding the physical body, a peripheral organization that has a definite cosmic orientation is maintained throughout pregnancy and only partly submits to the laws of the physical world. The placental membranes neither join into the mineralization processes— beginning after the seventh week following conception, at the time of the transition from embryo to fetus, when osteogenesis is initiated— nor take part in the polar development of the sexual organization.[123] The placenta surrounding the child is connected with its higher members and is related to its cosmic-spiritual orientation and origin. It keeps its distance from earthly forces (from the "human participation in the earthly element"[124]) and fulfils its important task until the moment of birth, when the child begins to breathe and arrives in the physical world. Before birth, the human being is still "in the custody" of beings that stand above the physical[125]—living and growing in the womb, in a protected sphere,[126] and under a higher guidance. This "custody" cannot continue in the same way after birth and is transferred, at least in part, to the social realm of the parents, and becomes their responsibility.

This extra-embryonic organization enters the world as placental afterbirth and dies with the earthly birth of the child as the "corpse" of the previous life of the past nine months.

Ancient wisdom knew of the cosmic origin of the human being, of our "unbornness," which precedes the transition into the earthly community. In the history of humankind, the placenta was held in high respect by advanced civilizations, which understood its spiritual significance as protector, helper and companion of the child on the way to earth. In the Old Testament it is referred to as the "little bundle of life."[127] Throughout centuries, if not millennia, it was buried with a special ritual as an essential aspect of human beings, of our origin and cosmic life before birth. Wolfgang Schad draws our attention to this, describing an Egyptian slate drawing from the end of the fourth pre-Christian millennium that depicts the pharaoh's mummified afterbirth being carried before him in a procession as part of his insignia. While the pharaoh represented the sun god in the old Egyptian mysteries, his mummified placenta represented the spirituality of the moon, or the lunar sphere; a burial site often consisted of two pyramids, the southern grave being that of the mummified placenta in which the divine spirit was revered.[128]

*

Rudolf Steiner pointed out that when we meet children, we experience "something emanating from the child's gaze that did not come into existence through birth, something that reveals the depths of the human soul." This is true for any child, and in the visual art for which Raphael was so particularly gifted: "If we look at the children in Raphael's Madonna paintings we see that something gazes at us out of the eyes of these children, something divine, mysterious and super-human, something that is still connected to a child for a time after the birth."[129]

This consciousness of—and reverence for—human existence before birth is of great significance for education and for the culture of life in the future: for a civilization that will begin once more to contemplate the life conditions of the individual and of the community.

Just as the memories of one's past life rise as a tableau before the soul just after death, a kind of preview of future life precedes the new incarnation. We do not see every detail, but a rough outline of all the circumstances of the life to come. This moment is immensely important. It can even happen that those who endured a great deal in an earlier life, and experienced great hardship, suffer a shock when they perceive their new situation and destiny, and therefore keep their soul from fully incarnating so that only a part of the soul enters into the body.[130]

In his anthroposophical and pedagogical lectures Rudolf Steiner repeatedly described how the experiences before conception and the life-processes of the human spirit-soul still reverberate during early child development when the child learns to stand upright and acquires the skills of walking, speaking, and thinking.[131] These same pre-conceptual experiences and spirit-soul life-processes also come to expression in the imitative relationship occurring between the child and the world in the first seven years of the child's development. During that time, children live devotedly and trustingly in their social environment; they take in what they perceive and they imitate it in a creative way, deeply absorbing the essence of the other person, their gestures, habits, and moral disposition. The special relationship that the young child enjoys with the surroundings—and that will never be experienced in this way again—does not arise after birth out of "nothing," nor is it the result of "learning" or "education." On the contrary, it precedes education and forms its foundation. It does so as a reverberation of life before conception in the spiritual world, of the intuitive encounters and relationships that took place before the transition from the spiritual to the earthly community, and in fact made this transition possible:

Imitation is basically the continuation of what lived in a totally different form before birth or conception in the spiritual world, where all beings merge into one another; it comes to expression when the child imitates the human beings around him or her as a resonance of the spiritual experience.[132]

If we contemplate the life of the child in the right way we can see the streaming in and radiating of the life between death and a new birth.[133]

When, at Christmas 1920, Ita Wegman prepared for the opening, the "birth," of her clinic in Arlesheim, Rudolf Steiner presented the following verse to her:

We are a bridge
Between what is past
And future existence;
The present is an instant:
Is momentary bridge.
Spirit become soul
In enfolding matter
Is from the past;
Soul becoming spirit
In germinal vessels
Is on the path to the future.
Grasp what is to come
Through what is past;
Have hope of what is growing
Through what has emerged.
And so apprehend
Existence in growing;
And so apprehend
What is growing in what is.[134]

APPENDIX

Rudolf Steiner

The Transition from Cosmic to Earthly Existence in the Development of the Human Being

(1922)

While we sleep, as human beings, our physical and etheric organisms form an outer world for our soul-spirit being. They are available to us just as they are, over and over again, during the waking state, when they can become the instrument of our soul and spirit. We take the desire for these two organisms with us into sleep. This desire [...] is connected with the cosmic spiritual powers whose sensory image we see in the appearances of the moon. As human beings, we are subject to the lunar powers, but only through our being part of the earth. Contemplation of the condition before we turn toward earthly life—in which we find ourselves in the purely spiritual world for a certain time— makes it clear that there we are not subject during that time to the influences of the lunar powers.

In the purely spiritual state, we do not experience a physical and etheric human organism as belonging to us as we do when we are sleeping. We experience these organisms in a totally different way. We experience their foundations in cosmic worlds. We experience how these organisms evolve out of the spiritual cosmos. We behold a spiritual cosmos. This spiritual cosmos is the spiritual part of the germ of the physical earthly organism with which we will be united in future. When we speak of a germ in this context we are describing something that is the opposite of what we call a germ in the physical sense. Usually, when we speak of "germ" in this connection, we mean the minute physical beginning of a growing, expanding organism or structure. But the spiritual organism, made up of powers or forces, which one sees in one's pre-earthly spiritual existence in connection with one's essence, is huge and continually contracts, as it were, until finally it grows together with the physical germ.

We use the terms *huge* and *minute* in this context, but we must always bear in mind that the events in the spiritual world are spiritual. Space in the physical sense does not exist there. The terms are therefore used only as images for something spiritual, entirely non-spatial, and purely qualitative.

During pre-earthly existence, we experience the cosmic creation that is the spiritual germ of our future physical organism. And this spiritual creation is experienced as a unity with the entire spiritual cosmos, while at the same time revealing itself as the cosmic body of the human essence. We experience the spiritual cosmos as the powers of our own being. Our entire existence consists in that we experience *ourselves* in this cosmos. But we do not experience *only* ourselves. Unlike our future physical organism, this cosmic existence does not separate us from the rest of cosmic life. We experience this life as intuition. The life of the other spiritual beings is also *our* life.

As human beings, we live our pre-earthly existence in the active experience of the spirit-germ of our future physical organism. We ourselves prepare this organism in that we collaborate on the spirit-germ with other spiritual beings in the spiritual world. Just as in earthly life we perceive with our senses a physical environment in which we are active, we perceive how in our pre-earthly existence our physical organism is formed out of the spirit. We are actively involved in its formation, just as during our physical existence we participate actively in the formation of physical things in the world around us.

A whole universe, no less multiplicitous and diverse than the physical sensory world, is present in the spirit-germ of the physical human body that our spirit-soul witnesses during pre-earthly existence. Indeed, intuitive knowledge may well say that what human beings unconsciously carry within them, contracted into their physical form, is a universe of such magnificence that the physical world cannot be remotely compared with it.

It is *this* universe that we experience spiritually and on which we work in our pre-earthly existence. We experience its growing, its mobility, but filled with spiritual entities.

Within this world, we are conscious. Our own powers are related to the powers that are active in the unfolding of this universe. The collaboration of the spiritual cosmic powers with our own powers fills our consciousness. In a sense, the sleep state is an imitation of this activity. But in sleep this activity proceeds in such a way that the physical organism exists as a separate form, apart from the human spirit-soul. The active powers that form the content of pre-earthly human consciousness are absent. Therefore the sleep state unfolds unconsciously.

In the further course of pre-earthly existence, conscious experience of the growing future earthly organism is more and more dulled. It does not completely disappear, but it becomes faint. It is as if we felt increasingly alienated from our own cosmic inner world. We live ourselves out of that world. What used to be a complete oneness with cosmic spiritual beings now appears as a mere revelation of these beings. We might say that while previously we experienced the spiritual world as intuition, now we experience it as inspiration: that is, the cosmic essence now works on us from the outside, as revelation.

Employing expressions that illustrate the suprasensible by means of analogous relationships in physical experience, an experience now emerges in the human spirit-soul that could be described as a feeling of "deprivation," or as the arising of a "desire for things lost."

The human soul lives in this "deprivation" and "desire" at a later stage of pre-earthly existence. The soul then no longer experiences the full reality of living together with spiritual world, but experiences it only as a revealed reflection. In a certain way, then, one might say the spiritual world is less intensely present in consciousness.

The human soul next gains the maturity to experience with the spiritual lunar powers, which, until then, were outside its sphere of existence. Thereby it receives its being, in that, as an independent being, it separates itself from the other spiritual beings with whom it used to be united. We might say that it used to be permeated by the spirit and by God and that now it feels itself to be an independent soul being. The cosmos has become outer world, even though the experience of cosmic revelation is still very intense in the initial phase and is only dimmed down gradually.

In this experience, we progress from the spirit-permeated existence that we used to experience as reality to an existence in which we are confronted with the revelation of the spiritual cosmos. The first experience is the reality of what in later earthly existence appears as the soul's disposition for religious thought and feeling. The second experience is the reality of what, when it is described, provides a true cosmology, because the physical human organisation is contemplated with its cosmic genesis without which it remains incomprehensible.

In the following period, we lose our vision of the spiritual cosmos. It grows dark to our "spiritual eyes." Instead, we now experience our inner soul lives, which are more intimately connected with the spiritual moon forces, with greater intensity and gain the maturity to receive from the outside what we had experienced from within. The spiritual work on the evolving physical organism in which we were consciously involved before, falls away from the soul organs and is transformed into the physical activity needed for the reproductive processes on the earth. What the human soul experienced before is transferred to these reproductive processes to become their directing powers. The human soul then lives for some time in the spiritual world without being involved in the development of the physical human organism.

During this stage the soul develops the maturity to satisfy

its sense of "deprivation" and "desire" in the etheric world of the cosmos. It draws the cosmic ether toward itself and forms its etheric organism in accordance with the foundations gained when working on the human universe. In this way, we live ourselves into our etheric organism before our physical organism receives it in earthly existence.

The processes that follow conception bring the germinal physical processes to completion separated from the course of the human soul's last stages of pre-earthly life. The human soul has now integrated its etheric organism and is able to unite with the physical germ due to the powerful "desire" that it still experiences. With this union, the human being enters into physical earthly existence.

What the human soul experiences when it integrates its etheric organism—that is, when its etheric organism in a certain sense grows into it from the world ether—is an experience alien to earthly experience because it happens without the physical organism. But the physical organism is its "desired" object. What the infant experiences very early in life is an unconscious memory of this experience. But it is an *active* memory, an unconscious working on the physical organism—which used to be the inner world of the soul and which is now outside it. The formative activity, which the human being unconsciously performs on his or her own growing organism, is the outer manifestation of this active memory.[135]

Notes

[Translator's note: In the following references to the works of Rudolf Steiner, the page numbers refer to the German editions (GA). Passages have been newly translated to give consistency of terminology.]

1   GA 297, p. 206.
2   GA 40, p. 270.
3   GA 297a, pp. 123.
4   GA 335, p. 260.
5   For Rudolf Steiner's spiritual-scientific research method cf. his fundamental writings, e.g., the introductory chapter to his medical textbook (written in collaboration with the physician Ita Wegman): *Extending Practical Medicine. Fundamental Principles Based on the Science of the Spirit*, GA 27, tr. A. Meuss. (Chapter I: "Understanding the True Nature of Man as a Basis of Medical Practice").
6   GA 140, p. 170.
7   GA 40, p.169; English translation taken from: Rudolf Steiner: *Verses and Meditations*, Rudolf Steiner Press 2004 (revised by D.S. Osmond and C. Davy), p. 157.
8   "We have come into the world as beings for whom birth was just a transformation and equally we will leave the earthly world by going through death which is not the end but a transformation" (GA 236, p. 200).
9   GA 205, p. 80.
10   GA 239, p. 128.
11   GA 203, p. 274.
12   On March 13, 1921, Rudolf Steiner said in Dornach: "We must have a word that clearly designates pre-existence. One must not underestimate the importance that lies in the word. No matter how much we think or how astute our thinking,

there is something in us that is simply intellectual. As soon as a thought is expressed in a word, even if we only think the word, as in a word meditation, the word imprints itself in the world ether. The thought itself is not imprinted in the world ether as that would mean that we could not be free in pure thinking. The moment something is imprinted we become fixed, because we are not free in the word, but in pure thinking (you can read about this in more detail in my *Philosophy of Freedom*). The word is imprinted in the world ether. Now consider this: The situation for the science of initiation today is that, due to the fact that the civilized languages have no word for unbornness, this unbornness which is so important for humankind, is not imprinted in the world ether. All the important words that relate to the human being's origin, childhood, and youth, are terrible for the ahrimanic powers. Immortality written into the world ether is very pleasant for the ahrimanic powers, because immortality means that they want to begin a new creation with the human being and that they want to set forth with the human being. It is not at all irritating for the ahrimanic beings, as they keep whizzing through the ether to toy with human beings whenever the word immortality resounds again from the pulpits and is imprinted in the world ether. The ahrimanic beings revel in this. But it is a great horror to them when they find the word "unbornness" imprinted in the world ether. It puts out the light in which they move. They become stuck; they lose their orientation. It is as if an abyss opened beneath them. This shows that the ahrimanic beings are trying to keep humanity from speaking of unbornness. However paradoxical it might seem to modern human beings when one speaks to them of these things, modern civilization must speak of them. [...] It is in fact nothing less than the fight against the ahrimanic powers, which we must take upon us" (GA 203, pp. 274).

13   Letter to Madeleine van Deventer, Ita Wegman Archives (Arlesheim). Cf. also Peter Selg: *Die letzten drei Jahre. Ita Wegman in Ascona*. Dornach 2004, p. 51.

14 A comprehensive publication that includes all the different descriptions by Rudolf Steiner about the life of the soul between death and a new birth is not yet available, although he indirectly hinted at the need for this in 1923. ("All these things have to be collected by and by. Nobody should be able to say: Well, he described the passage of the human being through the time between death and a new birth first in this way and then in that way! If one visits a town, the first time, a second time, and so on, one will also describe things differently as one gets to know the place better. One has to bring the details together in a synopsis. It is the same here: the different descriptions of the human experience of the supersensible world must be collected, compared, and summarized. Only then will it be possible to gain an impression of what the supersensible world is like and how it is experienced by the human being" (GA 231, pp. 11). Publications on this theme that are available so far—including Elisabeth Vreede's "Das Leben zwischen Tod und neuer Geburt im Lichte der Astrologie. Part 1 to 3." In: *Anthroposophie und Astronomie*. Freiburg 1954, p. 165-190. (*Astronomy and Spiritual Science. The Astronomical Letters of Elisabeth Vreede*. Ed. Norman Davidson. Great Barrington, MA 2001. English translation by Ronald Koetzsch and Anne Riegel.) and Max Hoffmeister's *Die übersinnliche Vorbereitung der Inkarnation*. Basel 1979—refer only to certain aspects of the broad vista opened up by Rudolf Steiner.

15 Christian Morgenstern: *Werke und Briefe*. Stuttgart edition with commentary (StA), volume II. Lyrik 1887–1905. Ed. Martin Kiessig. Stuttgart 1988, p. 67. English translation by Matthew Barton and Margot Saar.

16 Theodor Hetzer (1890-1946), a German art historian highly respected for his expertise on the paintings of Giotto, Titian, and Raphael. In: *Die Sixtinische Madonna*. Frankfurt/Main 1947, p. 73.

17 "Das Bild der Andacht." Quoted from Michael Ladwein: *Raffaels Sixtinische Madonna. Literarische Zeugnisse aus zwei Jahrhunderten*. Dornach 2004, p. 35. English translation by Matthew Barton.

18   "Fece a' monaci Neri di San Sisto in Piacenza la tavola dello
     altar maggiore, dentrovi la Nostra Donna con San Sisto e
     Barbara...." (Giorgio Vasari, 1550; quoted from Marielene
     Putscher: *Raphaels Sixtinische Madonna.* Tübingen 1955,
     p. 4).
19   Theodor Hetzer: *Die Sixtinische Madonna,* p. 17.
20   Ibid., p. 69.
21   *"Die höchste Liebe wie die höchste Kunst ist Andacht."*
     Quoted from Michael Ladwein: *Raffaels Sixtinische
     Madonna. Literarische Zeugnisse aus zwei Jahrhunderten,*
     p. 35. English translation by Matthew Barton.
22   Andreas Henning: Raffael in Rom und die Entstehung der
     Sixtinischen Madonna. In: Claudia Brink and Andreas Henning
     (eds): *Raffael. Die Sixtinische Madonna. Geschichte und
     Mythos eines Meisterwerkes.* Munich and Berlin 2005, p. 15.
23   Quoted from Michael Ladwein: *Raffaels Sixtinische Madonna.
     Literarische Zeugnisse aus zwei Jahrhunderten,* p. 127.
24   Theodor Hetzer: *Die Sixtinische Madonna,* p. 68.
25   Ibid., p. 126.
26   Ibid., p. 132.
27   Marielene Putscher: *Raphaels Sixtinische Madonna,* p. 31.
28   Theodor Hetzer: *Die Sixtinische Madonna,* p. 66.
29   Quoted from Michael Ladwein: *Raffaels Sixtinische Madonna.
     Literarische Zeugnisse aus zwei Jahrhunderten,* p. 152.
30   Theodor Hetzer: *Die Sixtinische Madonna,* p. 12. Marielene
     Putscher wrote in relation to this: "The idea of the earth
     appearing beneath the clouds and Mary touching on it with
     her feet is compelling. Yet if one looks more closely there is
     no sign of the globe. Karl Morgenstern, who was among the
     first to describe the Sistine Madonna, drew attention to this
     remarkable phenomenon: Mary is 'the queen of the earth.
     Raphael subtly suggests her reign over the earth. How? The
     saint's yellow cloak is thrown back, its tail forming a circle
     segment that could not appear so definite and rounded if the
     corner of the garment was not resting on a sphere. Also, the
     way the remaining left side of the red-lined cloak is draped,
     the way the Madonna puts down her foot, and the way

the shadow of the clouds to her left is fashioned, all of this evokes in us the involuntary image of the earthly sphere covered by clouds on which the blessed mother, the holy virgin, is walking. Without employing hard definitions that would have destroyed the tender, airy imagination, the inspired artist subtly suggested something that those intent on following his intuition can easily discover.' More than Morgenstern says here, cannot—must not—be said. But it is enough. As soon as something definite is claimed it will be wrong" (p. 73 f.).

31 Arthur Schopenhauer: *Parerga and Paralipomena. Short philosophical essays.* Oxford 1974, p. 665. English translation by E.F.Y. Payne.

32 Michael Ladwein: *Raffaels Sixtinische Madonna. Literarische Zeugnisse aus zwei Jahrhunderten*, p. 152.

33 Ibid., p. 116.

34 Theodor Hetzer: *Die Sixtinische Madonna*, p. 10.

35 Quoted from Michael Ladwein: *Raffaels Sixtinische Madonna. Literarische Zeugnisse aus zwei Jahrhunderten*, p. 153.

36 Theodor Hetzer: *Die Sixtinische Madonna*, p. 13. ("Like sun and moon, the two faces relate to each other, and something essential lies in this comparison. In an early painting of the crucifixion, which is in the National Gallery in London, we see sun and moon, in the medieval manner, on either side of the cross; Raphael's primordial relationship to the forms of the universe streamed already then into the still symbolic presentation. Now, at the height of his creative power, this primordial essence permeated the human form and human life; the cosmic element is personified and, in the purified human being, it is raised to divinity. Everything that could be symbolic, abstract and immense has been transformed into gentleness and majesty; but we must not forget for a moment that it exists" Ibid.).

37 Quoted from Michael Ladwein: *Raffaels Sixtinische Madonna. Literarische Zeugnisse aus zwei Jahrhunderten*, p. 135.

38 Wilhelm Kelber: *Raffael von Urbino. Leben und Werk.* Stuttgart 1979, p. 389. Hetzer's statement from 1943 I find equally valid: 'Where Raphael creates such greatness and

purity as in the face of the Madonna, we must see Mary as the main figure; only in association with the face of the mother that of the child truly comes to life. Denying this means to interpret against what is obvious" (Theodor Hetzer: *Die Sixtinische Madonna*, p. 15).

39   Quoted from Michael Ladwein: *Raffaels Sixtinische Madonna. Literarische Zeugnisse aus zwei Jahrhunderten*, p. 34.

40   Ibid., p. 50.

41   Ibid., p. 91.

42   —Even if the central figure of the Sistine child transcends the human realm in certain respects since he is the (future) bearer of the cosmic Christ essence: "If we look at the children in Raphael's Madonna paintings we see that something gazes at us out of the eyes of the children, something divine, mysterious and super-human that still lives in children for a time after birth. This is visible in all of Raphael's images of children with one exception. One child image cannot be interpreted in this way: the Jesus child in the Sistine Madonna. If one looks into the eyes of this child, one knows that there is more in the eyes of this child than there can be in a human being. Raphael made this distinction: that in this one child of the Sistine Madonna there lives something purely spiritual, something Christ-like" (GA 143, p. 179).

43   GA 105, p. 23.

44   GA 202, p. 32.

45   GA 343, p. 227.

46   GA 62, p. 301.

47   GA 262, p. 125.

48   Wilhelm Kelber: *Raffael von Urbino*, p. 389.

49   GA 112, p. 20.

50   GA 62, p. 303.

51   Quoted from Michael Ladwein: *Raffaels Sixtinische Madonna. Literarische Zeugnisse aus zwei Jahrhunderten*, p. 110.

52   Eduard Lenz: *Gelebte Zukunft: Briefe, Aufsätze, Dokumente*. Stuttgart 1982, p. 100 f.

53   Cf. Uta Neidhardt: Die Dresdener Gemäldegalerien. Alte und neue Meister seit 1939. Auslagerung, Abtransport und

Rückkehr ihrer Werke. In: Staatliche Kunstsammlung Dresden (ed.): *Zurück in Dresden. Eine Ausstellung ehemals vermisster Werke aus Dresener Museen*. Dresden 1998.

54 Ruth Kranz-Löber: *"In der Tiefe des Hohlwegs." Die Shoah in der Lyrik von Nelly Sachs*. Würzburg 2001, p. 47.

55 Nelly Sachs: *Fahrt ins Staublose*. Frankfurt 1961, p. 67. English translation by Matthew Barton.

56 Quoted from Marielene Putscher: *Raphaels Sixtinische Madonna*. Tübingen 1955, p. 1.

57 Cf. Peter Selg: "In den Wohnungen des Todes." Erinnerung an Nelly Sachs (1891-1970). In Peter Selg: *"Alles ist unvergessen." Paul Celan und Nelly Sachs*. Dornach 2008, p. 21-138.

58 GA 231, p. 125.

59 GA 192, p. 251.

60 GA 135, *Wiederverkörperung und Karma und ihre Bedeutung für die Kultur der Gegenwart*.

61 GA 9, p. 88.

62 Ibid.

63 Christian Morgenstern: *Werke und Briefe*. StA Vol. II, p. 511. English translation by Matthew Barton.

64 GA 302, p. 138.

65 Rainer Maria Rilke: *Die Gedichte*. Frankfurt a.M. 1987, pp. 631. With regard to the circumstances of this verse cf. also Peter Selg: *Rainer Maria Rilke und Franz Kafka. Lebensweg und Krankheitsschicksal im 20. Jahrhundert*. Dornach 2007, pp. 31. English translation by A.S. Kilne.

66 Cf. Peter Selg: "In Christo Morimur." Der nachtodliche Weg der Menschenseele. In: Peter Selg: *Rudolf Steiners Totengedenken. Die Verstorbenen, der Dornacher Bau und die Anthroposophische Gesellschaft*. Arlesheim 2008, pp. 111-135.

67 GA 239, p. 82.

68 Ibid., p. 87.

69 Ibid., p. 89.

70 Ibid., p. 155.

71 Ibid., p. 102.

72 Ibid., p. 104.

73 GA 240, p. 126.

74 GA 218, pp. 115/289. In many of his lectures Rudolf Steiner spoke about the uniqueness, the extraordinary—microcosmic as well as macrocosmic—dimension of the human body. In May 1923, he said, in connection to the life of the human soul after death and the creation of the "spirit-germ" in the Sun sphere: "It is wonderful what we perceive when, for instance, we admire a beautiful landscape. It is wonderful what we perceive when we admire the starry heavens at night in all their grandeur. Yet, inside the human body, if we do not look at it with the anatomist's physical eye but with a spiritual eye, if we look at a human lung, a human liver, with a spiritual eye, there are entire worlds rolled together. Compared to the outer splendor and majesty of rivers and mountains, of the earthly world, all that is inside the human skin—as our physical organization—is much greater and more majestic. It makes no difference that it appears so much smaller than the vast universe. If you see what is in one single alveolus: it is much more magnificent than the mightiest Alpine mountain range. What is inside the human body is a condensation of the entire spiritual cosmos. In the human organization we have an image of the entire cosmos" (GA 226, p. 33f.).

75 GA 226, p. 36f.

76 GA 231, p. 106.

77 GA 226, p. 35.

78 GA 215, p. 98.

79 GA 25, p. 49.

80 GA 235, p. 137.

81 GA 239, p. 111.

82 GA 226, p. 24; author's emphasis.

83 GA 202, p. 95.

84 GA 226, p. 25.

85 GA 226, p. 38.

86 Ibid., p. 39.

87 GA 258, p. 14f.

88 GA 167, p. 41f.
89 GA 141, p. 143.
90 GA 63, p. 349.
91 GA 109, p. 204.
92 Ibid.
93 Cf. Peter Selg: *Krankheit, Heilung und Schicksal des Menschen. Über Rudolf Steiners geisteswissenschaftliches Pathologie- und Therapieverständnis*, p. 89f.
94 GA 140, p. 354f.
95 GA 343, p. 256.
96 Cf. GA 348, p. 144.
97 Cf. Rudolf Steiner's numerous descriptions of this process in Peter Selg (ed.): *Rudolf Steiner. Quellentexte für die Wissenschaften. Texte zur Medizin*. Volume 3: *Physiologische Menschenkunde*, pp. 114-118.
98 GA 343, p. 175.
99 GA 226, p. 36.
100 GA 201, p. 122.
101 GA 208, p. 204.
102 GA 227, p. 249.
103 GA 226, p. 39.
104 GA 218, p. 172.
105 GA 215, p. 104.
106 GA 226, p. 40.
107 GA 240, p. 17.
108 Ibid., p. 127.
109 GA 93a, p. 159.
110 GA 95, p. 52f.
111 GA 99, p. 38f.
112 cf. GA 95, p. 52f.
113 GA 218, p. 298.
114 Ibid.
115 GA 99, p. 55.
116 GA 316, p. 147.
117 GA 343, p. 256.
118 Cf. Peter Selg: *Vom Logos menschlicher Physis*. Volume 2, pp. 691.

119 "At the moment of death, the connection between the ether body and the astral body on the one hand, and the physical body on the other, is *dissolved in the heart.* There is a lighting up in the heart and then ether body, astral body, and the I lift out above the head" (GA 95, p. 28; author's emphasis).

120 Cf. Peter Selg: *Mysterium cordis. Studien zur sakramentalen Physiologie des Herzorgans. Aristoteles – Thomas von Aquin – Rudolf Steiner*, p. 23f.

121 GA 317, p. 32.

122 GA 226, p. 40.

123 Cf. Wolfgang Schad: Einführung. In: Wolfgang Schad (ed.): *Die verlorene Hälfte des Menschen. Die Plazenta vor und nach der Geburt in Medizin, Anthroposophie und Ethnologie*, p. 12f.

124 GA 343, p. 176.

125 GA 293, p. 22.

126 "What happens in the maternal uterus is protected from the forces of the earth. You must imagine the uterus as an organ which closes off the space, which does not allow the earthly influences to enter, so that the space is set aside for cosmic influences. We have a space which is directly connected to the cosmos, where cosmic influences take effect" (GA 317, p. 121f.).

127 5 Moses 28; 57 and 1 Samuel 25; 29. Cf. Wolfgang Schad: "Zur Anthropologie der Bekleidung. Der Mensch vor und nach der Geburt." In: Wolfgang Schad (ed.): *Die verlorene Hälfte des Menschen. Die Plazenta vor und nach der Geburt in Medizin, Anthroposophie und Ethnologie*, p. 63.

128 Cf. Wolfgang Schad: "Die Bedeutung der Nachgeburt in anthroposophischer Sicht." Ibid. p. 74/63 (Fig. 13).

129 GA 143, p. 179.

130 GA 296, p. 75.

131 Cf. GA 226, lectures of May 17 and 18, 1923.

132 GA 200, p. 115.

133 Ibid.; cf. also Peter Selg: *The Therapeutic Eye. How Rudolf Steiner Observed Children.* SteinerBooks 2008. English translation by Anna Meuss, Margot Saar.

134 Ita Wegman Archives, Arlesheim. Cf. also Facsimile print on p. ii of this volume. English translation by Matthew Barton.
135 From: Rudolf Steiner: *Drei Schritte der Anthroposophie. Philosophie – Kosmologie – Religion.* GA 25. Dornach 1999, pp. 47-53.

Literature Cited

Works by Rudolf Steiner, referred to in the text and notes. The German titles are from the Rudolf Steiner Gesamtausgabe (GA) published by Rudolf Steiner Verlag, Dornach, Switzerland.

GA 9   *Theosophy.* Tr. Catherine Creeger. Great Barrington, MA: SteinerBooks 2006. *Theosophie. Einführung in übersinnliche Welterkenntnis und Menschenbestimmung* (1904): 32. Auflage 2003.

GA 25   *Drei Schritte der Anthroposophie. Philosophie–Kosmologie–Religion* [Three steps of anthroposophy. philosophy–cosmology–religion] (1922): 4. Auflage 1999. (See also GA 215, in English: *Philosophy, Cosmology, Religion.* Spring Valley, NY: Anthroposophic Press 1984).

GA 40   *Truth-Wrought-Words.* Tr. Arvia MacKaye Ege. Spring Valley, NY: Anthroposophic Press 1979. *Wahrspruchworte* (1886–1925): 9. Auflage 2005.

GA 62   *Ergebnisse der Geistesforschung* [Results of spiritual research] (1912/13): 2. Auflage 1988.

GA 63   *Geisteswissenschaft als Lebensgut* [Spiritual science as a treasure for life] (1913/14): 2. Auflage 1986.

GA 93a   *Grundelemente der Esoterik* [Fundamentals of esotericism] (1905): 3. Auflage 1987.

GA 95   *Founding a Science of the Spirit.* [Originally: *At the Gates of Spiritual Science.*] Tr. E.H.G. and C.D. Revised by Matthew Barton. Forest Row, England: Rudolf Steiner Press 1999. *Vor dem Tore der Theosophie* (1906): 4. Auflage 1990.

GA 99   *Rosicrucian Wisdom. An Introduction.* Tr. J Collis. Forest Row, England: Rudolf Steiner Press 2000. *Die Theosophie des Rosenkreuzers* (1907): 7. Auflage 1985.

GA 105   *Universe, Earth, and Man.* Tr. Not known. Abridged from the German GA edition. London: Rudolf Steiner Press 1987. *Welt, Erde und Mensch* (1908): 5. Auflage 1983.

GA 109   *The Principle of Spiritual Economy. In Connection with Questions of Reincarnation.* Tr. Peter Mollenhauer. Hudson, NY: Anthroposophic Press 1986. *Das Prinzip der spirituellen Ökonomie in Zusammenhang mit Wiederverkörperungsfragen* (1909): 3. Auflage 2003.

GA 112   *The Gospel of St. John and Its Relation to the Other Gospels.* Tr. Samuel and Loni Lockwood, revised by Maria St. Goar. Great Barrington, MA: SteinerBooks. *Das Johannes-Evangelium im Verhältnis zu den drei anderen Evangelien* (1909): 6. Auflage 1984.

GA 135   *Reincarnation and Karma. Two Fundamental Truths of Human Existence.* Tr. D.S. Osmond, C. Davy, and S. and E.F. Derry. Great Barrington, MA: Anthroposophic Press 1992. *Wiederverkörperung und Karma und ihre Bedeutung für Kultur der Gegenwart* (1912): 5. Auflage 1961.

GA 140   *Life between Death and Rebirth.* Tr. R. M. Querido. Great Barrington, MA: SteinerBooks 2010. *Okkulte Untersuchungen über das Leben zwischen Tod und neuer Geburt* (1912/13): 5. Auflage 2003.

GA 143   *Erfahrungen des Übersinnlichen. Die drei Wege der Seele zu Christus* [Experiences of the Supersensible] (1912): 4. Auflage 1994.

GA 167   *Gegenwärtiges und Vergangenes im Menschengeiste* [The present and the past in the human spirit] (1916): 2. Auflage 1962.

GA 192   *Geisteswissenschaftliche Behandlung sozialer und pädagogischer Fragen* [Spiritual-scientific treatment of social and pedagogical questions] (1919): 2. Auflage 1991.

GA 200   *The New Spirituality and the Christ Experience of the Twentieth Century.* Tr. Paul King. Hudson, NY: Anthroposophic Press 1988. *Die neue Geistigkeit und das Christus-Erlebnis des zwanzigsten Jahrhunderts* (1920): 4. Auflage 2003.

GA 201 *The Mystery of the Universe*. Tr. revised by Matthew Barton. Forest Row, England: Rudolf Steiner Press 2001. *Entsprechungen zwischen Mikrokosmos und Makrokosmos* (1920): 2. Auflage 1987.

GA 202 *The Bridge Between Universal Spirituality and the Physical Constitution of Man*. Tr. D.S. Osmond. Great Barrington, MA: SteinerBooks 2007. *Die Brücke zwischen der Weltgeistigkeit und dem Physischen des Menschen* (1920): 4. Auflage 1993.

GA 203 *Die Verantwortung des Menschen für die Weltentwickelung* [The responsibility of human beings for the development of the world through their spiritual connection to the earth and the world of the stars] (1921): 2. Auflage 1989.

GA 205 *Menschenwerden, Weltenseele und Weltengeist, erster Teil* [Human development, world-soul and world-spirit] (1921): 2. Auflage 1987.

GA 208 *Cosmosophy, Vol 2. Cosmic Influences on the Human Being*. Tr. A.R. Muess. Australia: Completion Press 1985. *Anthroposophie als Kosmosophie, zweiter Teil* (1921): 3. Auflage 1992.

GA 215 *Philosophy, Cosmology and Religion*. Tr. Lisa D. Monges and Doris M. Bugbey, revised by Maria St. Goar. Spring Valley, NY: Anthroposophic Press 1984. *Die Philosophie, Kosmologie und Religion in der Anthroposophie* (1922): 2. Auflage 1980.

GA 218 *Waldorf Education and Anthroposophy Vol. 2*. Tr. Nancy Parsons Whittaker, Robert Lathe, and Roland Everett. Hudson, NY: Anthroposophic Press 1996. *Geistige Zusammenhänge in der Gestaltung des menschlichen Organismus* (1922): 6. Auflage 1994.

GA 226 *Man's Being, His Destiny, and World-Evolution*. Tr. Erna McArthur. Spring Valley, NY: Anthroposophic Press 1984. *Menschenwerden, Menschenschicksal und Welt-Ent-wickelung* (1923): 5. Auflage 1988.

GA 227 *The Evolution of Consciousness as Revealed through Initiation-Knowledge*. Tr. V.E. Watkin and C. Davy.

Revised by Rudolf Steiner Press. Forest Row, England: Rudolf Steiner Press 2007. *Initiations-Erkenntnis* (1923): 4. Auflage 2000.

GA 231 *At Home in the Universe. Exploring Our Suprasenory Nature.* Tr. H. Collison. Revised by Anthroposophic Press. Hudson, NY: Anthroposophic Press 2000. *Der übersinnliche Mensch, anthroposophisch erfasst* (1923): 4. Auflage 1999.

GA 235 *Karmic Relationships. Esoteric Studies. Vol. I.* Tr. George Adams. Revised by M. Cotterell, C. Davy, and D.S. Osmond. London: Rudolf Steiner Press 1997. *Esoterische Betrachtungen karmischer Zusammenhänge. Erster Band* (1924): 8. Auflage 1994.

GA 239 *Karmic Relationships. Esoteric Studies. Vol. V.* Tr. D.S. Osmond. London: Rudolf Steiner Press 1997. *Esoterische Betrachtungen karmischer Zusammenhänge. Fünfter Band* (1924): 3. Auflage 1985.

GA 240 *Karmic Relationships. Esoteric Studies. Vol. VI.* Tr. and revised D.S.O., E.H.G. and M.K. London: Rudolf Steiner Press 1989. *Esoterische Betrachtungen karmischer Zusammenhänge. Sechster Band* (1924): 5. Auflage 1992.

GA 258 *The Anthroposophic Movement.* Tr. Christian von Arnim. Bristol, England: Rudolf Steiner Press 1993. *Die Geschichte und die Bedingungen der anthroposophischen Bewegung im Verhältnis zur Anthroposophischen Gesellschaft* (1923): 3. Auflage 1981.

GA 262 *Correspondence and Documents 1901–1925.* Tr. Christian and Ingrid von Arnim. Hudson, NY: Anthroposophic Press 1988. *Rudolf Steiner/Marie Steiner-von Sivers: Briefwechsel und Dokumente* (1901–1925): 2. Auflage 2002.

GA 293 *The Foundations of Human Experience.* Tr. Robert Lathe and Nancy Parsons Whittaker. Hudson, NY: Anthroposophic Press 1996. [See also *Study of Man*] *Allgemeine Menschenkunde als Grundlage der Pädagogik* (1919): 9. Auflage 1992.

GA 296   *Education as a Force for Social Change.* Tr. Robert Lathe and Nancy Parsons Whittaker. Hudson, NY: Anthroposophic Press 1997. *Die Erziehungsfrage als soziale Frage* (1919): 4. Auflage 1991.

GA 297   *The Spirit of the Waldorf School.* Robert Lathe and Nancy Parsons Whittaker. Hudson, NY: Anthroposophic Press 1995. *Idee und Praxis der Waldorfschule* (1920): 1. Auflage 1998.

GA 297a   *Erziehung zum Leben* [Education for life] (1921-24): 1. Auflage 1998.

GA 302   *Education for Adolescents.* Tr. Carl Hoffmann. Hudson, NY: Anthroposophic Press 1996. *Menschenerkenntnis und Unterrichtsgestaltung* (1921): 5. Auflage 1986.

GA 316   *Course for Young Doctors.* Spring Valley, NY: Mercury Press 1997. *Meditative Betrachtungen und Anleitungen zur Vertiefung der Heilkunst* (1924): 4. Auflage 2003.

GA 317   *Education for Special Needs. The Curative Education Course.* Tr. Mary Adams. Revised by Rudolf Steiner Press. London: Rudolf Steiner Press 1998. *Heilpädagogischer Kurs* (1924): 8. Auflage 1985.

GA 335   *Die Krisis der Gegenwart und der Weg des gesunden Denkens* [The crisis of the present and the path to healthy thinking] (1920): 1. Auflage 2005.

GA 343   *Vorträge und Kurse über christlich-religiöses Wirken, II* [Lectures and courses on christian religious work, vol. 2] (1921): 1. Auflage 1993.

GA 348   *From Comets to Cocaine.* [Originally published as *Health and Illness, Vol. 1 and 2.* Tr. Maria St. Goar] Tr. revised by Matthew Barton. London: Rudolf Steiner Press 2000. *Über Gesundheit und Krankheit* (1922/23): 3. Auflage 1983.

Secondary Literature

HOFFMEISTER, MAX: *Die übersinnliche Vorbereitung der Inkarnation.* Basel 1979.

SCHAD, WOLFANG (Hg.): *Die verlorene Hälfte des Menschen. Die Plazenta vor und nach der Geburt in Medizin, Anthroposophie und Ethnologie.* Stuttgart 2005.

SELG, PETER: *Vom Logos menschlicher Physis. Die Entfaltung einer anthroposophischen Humanphysiologie im Werk Rudolf Steiners.* 2 Bände. Dornach 2006.

— *Mysterium cordis. Studien zu einer sakramentalen Physiologie des Herzorganes. Aristoteles–Thomas von Aquin–Rudolf Steiner.* Dornach 22005.

— (Hg.): *Rudolf Steiner. Quellentexte für die Wissenschaften. Texte zur Medizin. Band 3. Physiologische Menschenkunde.* Dornach 2004.

— *Krankheit, Heilung und Schicksal des Menschen. Über Rudolf Steiners geisteswissenschaftliches Pathologie- und Therapieverständnis.* Dornach 2004.

— *The Therapeutic Eye. How Rudolf Steiner Observed Children.* Tr. Anna Meuss, Margot Saar. Great Barrington, MA: SteinerBooks 2008. *Der therapeutische Blick. Rudolf Steiner sieht Kinder.* Dornach 2005.

VREEDE, ELISABETH: "Das Leben zwischen Tod und neuer Geburt im Lichte der Astrologie." Teil 1 bis 3. In: *Anthroposophie und Astronomie.* Freiburg 1954, S. 165–190. [See *Astronomy and Spiritual Science. The Astronomical letters of Elisabeth Vreede.* Tr. Anne Riegel and Ronald Koetzsch. Great Barrington, MA: SteinerBooks 2001].

Ita Wegman Institute
for Basic Research into Anthroposophy

PFEFFINGER WEG 1 A CH-4144 ARLESHEIM, SWITZERLAND
www.wegmaninstitut.ch
e-mail: sekretariat@wegmaninstitut.ch

The Ita Wegman Institute for Basic Research into Anthroposophy is a non-profit research and teaching organization. It undertakes basic research into the lifework of Dr. Rudolf Steiner (1861–1925) and the application of anthroposophy in specific areas of life, especially medicine, education, and curative education. Work carried out by the Institute is supported by a number of foundations and organizations and an international group of friends and supporters. The Director of the Institute is Prof. Dr. Peter Selg.

CPSIA information can be obtained at www.ICGtesting.com
Printed in the USA
BVOW061929080512

289644BV00001B/2/P